choose
a changed mind

anita pearce

CHOOSE A CHANGED MIND
Copyright © 2013 by Anita Pearce

All rights reserved. Neither this publication nor any part of this publication may be reproduced or transmitted in any form or by any means, electronic or mechanical, including photocopying, recording or any information storage and retrieval system, without permission in writing from the author.

All Scripture quotations, unless otherwise specified, are from The Holy Bible, New International Version. Copyright 1973, 1978, 1984. International Bible Society. Used by permission of Zondervan Publishing House. All rights reserved. • Scriptures marked KJV are from The Holy Bible, King James Version. Copyright 1977, 1984. Thomas Nelson Inc., Publishers. • Scripture quotations marked NLT are taken from the Holy Bible, New Living Translation, copyright 1996. Used by permission of Tyndale House Publishers, Inc., Wheaton, Illinois 60189. All rights reserved.

I have attempted to give credit where credit is due. If something is not properly credited, this was not intentional. I do not necessarily endorse the theological perspectives of quoted authors.

Printed in Canada

ISBN: 978-1-4866-0146-2

Word Alive Press
131 Cordite Road, Winnipeg, MB R3W 1S1
www.wordalivepress.ca

WORD ALIVE PRESS
Just Write!

MIX
Paper from responsible sources
FSC® C016245

Cataloguing in Publication information may be obtained from Library and Archives Canada.

For more information, please contact:
Inspiration Ministries
Box 44
Margo, SK Canada S0A 2M0
www.inspirationministries.net

To you, the reader,
as you passionately follow Jesus Christ.

"Let this mind be in you, which was also in Christ Jesus."
Philippians 2:5 (KJV)

Acknowledgements	vii
Introduction	ix
one Recognizing the Power of Thought	1
two Realizing Personal Responsibility	15
three Relying on Spiritual Resources	27
four Refusing Poisonous Thoughts	45
five Renewing Thought Patterns	61
six Receiving Transformations	81
Conclusion	95
The Gift of Salvation	99
Endnotes	101

Acknowledgements

I have been blessed to partner with a network of remarkable friends. They are among the most precious treasures in my life. They continually motivate me to excellence. I wish to express particular appreciation to:

The board of Inspiration Ministries—for their encouragement, wise counsel, and friendship. Your support and vision for this ministry inspires and strengthens me.

Leanne Simpson—for typing out the original sermon. Your dependable assistance and consistently cheerful attitude are a blessing.

Darlene Kienle—for being my loyal friend and colleague. Your faithful friendship, genuine care, and personal integrity have inspired my courage, directing me ever closer to Jesus.

Alice Dutcyvich—for selflessly sharing hours of your time to review and revise this manuscript. I am deeply grateful for your patient counsel. Your pursuit of proper grammar and accurate details has turned coal into diamonds.

Doreen Holdsworth—for your keen editorial skills and creativity. Thank you for sharing your amazing ability to identify and clarify necessary changes.

Several friends—for reading the manuscript and offering valuable advice.

The Word Alive Press publishing team—for being so awesome. It has been a priviledge working with you.

Introduction

She was a wee wisp of a woman, not five feet tall and weighing less than ninety pounds. Her eyes sparkled with mischief. Her dry humor and quick wit kept me in stitches of laughter. Everyone was infected by her good cheer.

At one hundred years of age, Ruby was bright, sharp, and full of zip. She informed me that she was still a very good driver but had decided it was time to give up her license because, as she confided, "There are so many people who are bad drivers out there!"

When I commented on her great age, she laughed and replied, "Age is just a matter of mind. If you don't mind, it doesn't matter!" She continued, "We are never really old until we think we are."

* * *

Our thoughts exert powerful influence over every aspect of our lives. Our behavior is the result of our habitual thought patterns. If we desire to alter our conduct, we must take responsibility to change the way we think. God hasn't left us alone in this challenge but has given us effective tools to apply truth to our minds. There are practical steps we can follow to make change permanent and effectual.

We can make the choice to refuse negative and harmful thinking. It's important to take control of wandering thoughts and permit life-imparting meditations to take precedence. As we choose to let wholesome, God-centered thoughts rule our minds, they'll bring courage and transformation in our lives and character. We can choose a changed mind!

The ideas shared in these pages are the result of practical experience, personal observation, the wisdom of others, and common-sense inspiration. I do not assume to understand all the variants of mental conditions or psychological afflictions, including minds which may have been damaged by drugs or disease. There are those who may need intensive therapy and medication to assist in mental stability. It is my prayer, however, that you will find practical help to experience renewed, hope-filled thinking.

chapter one
Recognizing the Power of Thought

*You are not what you think you are,
but what you think, you are!*
Dr. David Jeremiah[1]

Man's greatness lies in his power of thought.
Blaise Pascal[2]

While recovering from a serious illness, a man was forced to lie flat on his back in the hospital for several long months. His long, tiresome days were brightened, however, by the cheerful stranger who shared his room.

His roommate had the bed beside the window. Every day he would describe in great detail all that was happening outside. He would talk for hours about the flowers of spring, the bird's nest in the nearby tree, and the crowds of bustling shoppers. One day he gave a description of a passing parade, even describing the bright costumes of the marching band. Even though he was daily getting weaker, his happy words brought encouragement to his bedridden comrade.

One morning, his newfound friend became deathly ill and was moved out of the room. The first man missed his friend's sunny disposition and optimistic chatter. He asked the nurses if he could be moved into the bed beside the window. Hoping to get just a glimpse of the wonderful world outside that had been so clearly described to him, he very slowly, painfully lifted himself to peek out the window.

To his absolute astonishment, he could see nothing but a solid brick wall. Shocked by his discovery, he called the nurse. He told her about his friend's daily description of the amazing world outside. The nurse explained that his friend had been completely blind.

Instead of complaint, his friend had chosen good cheer. All the lovely flowers, the birds, even the colorful parade had been created in a mind filled with beauty. He had shared the wonder of his imaginations to lift the heart of his comrade.[3]

Thoughts are powerful. The way we think determines the basic expressions of our identity, character, habits, and communication. Our reactions, our goals, even our motivations are decided by thought processes developed throughout our lives.

Consistently drawing from the resources provided by our senses, our brains busily calculate, categorize, and catalogue details, then determine responses. The

Eventually, certain habits of thought become the roots of our character.

accumulation of experiences, both past and present, provide material with which we govern our conduct. Eventually, certain habits of thought become the roots of our character.

Some may suppose that their cherished private meditations will have no effect on their daily lives. But every thought eventually will reproduce by influencing our health, character, and conduct. King Solomon observed that whatever people think will eventually be revealed. He wrote in Proverbs 23:7, *"For as he thinketh in his heart, so is he"* (KJV).

Some may try to change their external behavior without considering the root cause—lifestyles permitted and developed in the mind. An angry person expresses angry thoughts. Impure thinking can degenerate into promiscuity. Fear-filled reasoning produces anxiety, stress, and a whole horde of physical disorders.

Our thoughts are the controlling influences which determine our attitudes, emotions, words, and actions. They even impact our physical health. Whatever is going on in our minds will eventually be manifested outwardly.

Thoughts Influence Attitudes

Thinking negative thoughts will produce a negative mindset.

Our attitudes are directly impacted by our thoughts. We often say to our children, "Change your attitude!" Why do we say that? Because it is possible to change our attitudes. Thinking negative thoughts will produce a negative mindset. One look out the window on a rainy day and cultivated thought patterns can create a sour outlook! We may growl at the children, get irritated by the dog, or annoyed with phone calls. Everything seems glum and bleak. We feel cranky and cross.

However, if a good friend shows up at our door or we discover we have more money in our wallet than we thought, our whole demeanor can change instantly. This shift in our thoughts creates a radical change of attitude!

We have all crossed paths with those who live under a cloud of pessimism and gloom. No matter how many blessings are right in front of them, their attitudes exude criticism and discontent.

On some occasions, I confess to have had less than a stellar attitude. It usually happens when things don't go my way! One evening after a particularly hectic day, I was invited to meet with friends at a local coffee shop. I was tired and didn't want to go, but felt obligated to participate. I tried to disguise my grumpy attitude. As everyone excitedly chattered about their day, I just wanted to go home to bed. Other friends showed up. It was getting late.

Then I was introduced to the new lady who had just joined us. I realized I was in the company of a very famous person! My fatigue vanished. I could scarcely contain my excitement. My countenance glowed with the biggest smile I could produce. The realization that this well-known individual had come especially to meet me nearly knocked my socks off. I was thunderstruck! My attitude experienced an instant transformation because of the turnaround in my thoughts.

Thoughts Influence Emotions

Our thoughts have a powerful impact on our emotions. We're not always sure why we respond in certain ways. Closer observation usually reveals that our feelings are the result of what we've been thinking.

Suppose you're reminded of someone who hurt you deeply. Scars rip open as you once again hear that person's painful, cutting words. Your anger burns hot. You may even rehearse the sharp, witty retort you wish you could have given.

Suddenly, almost from nowhere, a very pleasant and kind man crosses the screen of your memory. You reflect on what a difficult and sad life he experienced and how tragic his early death. It was all so unfair. Sadness overwhelms you.

Just as quickly, your thoughts float to another acquaintance. She's the life of the party, a bundle of energy, full of laughter. Just remembering her sparkling eyes and quick wit cheers your heart. You may even laugh out loud as your mind replays an amusing conversation with her.

If we can bring order to our thoughts, our emotions will stabilize.

If we rewind the process, we discover that our wandering thoughts led our emotions from mad to sad to glad—all in two minutes!

You may say, "I cannot seem to control my emotions. I feel like I'm on an emotional roller coaster." Why do emotions experience such disturbances? It's because our thoughts are in turmoil. If we can bring order to our thoughts, our emotions will stabilize.

From time to time, a concern pops into my head just as I'm about to go to sleep. It will turn around and around in my mind all night if I let it. Sleep evaporates as I try to resolve the situation. Usually, however, if I get up and occupy my thoughts with a good book, prayer, or do something else for a few minutes, I can go back to bed and immediately drift off. The turmoil is settled by thinking about something else.

Circumstances may affect our emotions because we re-live the events in our minds. If we meditate on angry thoughts, we'll feel anger. If we concentrate on fear-filled happenings, we'll feel afraid. Conversely, if we change our perspective and think in another direction, our emotional state will also change.

> *What is in the well comes up in the bucket.*

Thoughts Influence Words

The way we think is also the source of the words we speak. It doesn't take long to discover what people are thinking; just listen to what they say.

We cannot think about one thing while talking about something else—at least not for very long. Our mental faculties are involved in the words we speak. Our preoccupations are soon revealed. As the old adage states, "What is in the well comes up in the bucket."

Of course, there are those who don't seem to think at all when they talk! Someone has said, "Some people put their brain into neutral and let their tongue idle on." Another wrote, "The bore kills time by talking it to death."

There are those who may be greatly concerned over what others say about them. What we say about ourselves is much more important! Any astute listener rapidly discerns what we think about ourselves, others, and God by listening to our words. Some folks continually put themselves down. They have difficulty accepting praise and will downgrade honest compliments. Their words show their low opinion of themselves.

Speech reveals pride or prejudice. It discloses fear, anger, and discouragement. Some individuals pour out a steady stream of complaint, vulgarity, or irritation. The true intents of the heart are plainly exposed by words.

One of my high school teachers had a small plaque on his desk that read, "It is better to remain silent and be thought a fool than to speak and remove all doubt!" Proverbs 17:28 gives us similar words of wisdom: *"Even a fool is thought wise if he keeps silent, and discerning if he holds his tongue."*

Then there are those delightful people who exude good cheer by their uplifting words. Gratitude, kindness, compassion fill their conversation.

What we think about will be heard in our speech. Someone commented, "Every time we speak, our hearts are on parade."

Thoughts Influence Actions

Our actions are consequences of our thoughts. With perhaps the exception of instinctual responses to danger or unforeseen circumstances, our deeds are the result of thought patterns. Jesus said in Matthew 15:19, *"For out of the heart come evil thoughts, murder, adultery, sexual immorality, theft, false testimony, slander."*

My friend's three-year-old son was full of energy. From early morning to evening, he zipped about playing, learning, and exploring. A general racket accompanied him. He would imitate tractors, trucks, and trains, as well as various animals. There was clamor and clatter—or shatter—wherever he went. When all fell silent, his mother immediately set off to find him. It was a clear sign of mischief. Sure enough, she would discover he was into something. On one occasion, he was perched on the dresser with a cape around his shoulders, ready to fly off as Superman! She could tell exactly what he was thinking by his actions.

Before committing a robbery, the thief plans the crime. Adultery grows out of an impure thought process. The action is the harvest of seeds that have been nurtured in the mind. If we desire to change the way we act, we must change the way we think.

Thoughts Influence Health

It has long been acknowledged that our physical well-being is deeply affected by the way we think. Dozens of diseases have been directly linked to psychosomatic causes.

Stress starts in the brain!

Everywhere we go, we hear warnings of the health risks linked to stress. But what is stress? Basically, it's a mind filled with anxiety or anger, often over uncontrollable events. Stress starts in the brain!

In an article discussing how thoughts affect our health, journalist Marlo Sollitto lists fifteen health problems directly associated with prolonged stress, including:

- Weakening of the immune system, making you more likely to have colds or other infections.
- High blood pressure.
- Upset stomach, ulcers, and acid reflux.
- Anxiety.
- Rapid heartbeat and heart palpitations.
- Panic attacks.
- Cardiovascular problems.
- Increased blood sugar levels.
- Irritable bowel problems.
- Backaches.

- Tension headaches or migraines.
- Sleep problems.
- Chronic fatigue syndrome.
- Respiratory problems and heavy breathing.
- Worsening of skin conditions, such as eczema.[4]

According to Dr. Caroline Leaf, the damage created by negative thoughts can be traced by disrupted chemical reactions in the brain. Harmful, stress-filled thoughts cause health issues because they promote a toxic mix and excessive release of potent chemicals.[5] The way we think has corresponding physical implications. The disastrous consequences of poisonous thoughts should challenge us to change the way we think!

It is astonishing to recognize the tremendous power, potential, and influence of our thoughts. They exert control over every aspect of our lives. Our attitudes and emotions, words, actions, and health are all directly influenced by our thinking processes. We must recognize the power of our thoughts and discover the transformation that can be experienced by bringing our minds under control.

Questions to Assist Practical Application

1. How have your thoughts influenced your attitudes?

2. Do your emotions seem out of control? Have you recognized the power your thoughts exert over your emotions?

3. What do your words reveal about you? Do you tend to put yourself down when speaking to others?

4. What thoughts have you tried to hide, hoping they won't be revealed by your attitudes, words, or actions?

5. How has your health been affected by the way you've been thinking?

6. Have you recognized the powerful influence your thoughts exert over your life?

Challenge

"Therefore, prepare your minds for action;
be self-controlled;
set your hope fully on the grace to be given you
when Jesus Christ is revealed."

1 Peter 1:13

chapter two
Realizing Personal Responsibility

A little kingdom I possess,
Where thoughts and feelings dwell,
And very hard the task I find
of governing it well.
Louisa May Alcott[6]

The man who sows wrong thoughts and deeds and
prays that God will bless him
is in the position of a farmer who,
having sown tares,
asks God to bring forth for him a harvest of wheat.
James Lane Allen[7]

It's one thing to recognize the formidable power of our thoughts. It is of paramount importance, however, to realize our individual responsibility in controlling and directing those thoughts. We think the thoughts we *choose* to think.

Choose A Changed Mind

We are completely responsible for the meditations and processes we allow into our brains. No one else can reach into our heads and control our thinking. Although our thoughts can be influenced by circumstances, environment, media, and even by other people, we alone make the final choice of which ones stay in our minds.

> *The person I'll be tomorrow will be the result of my choices today.*

As a teenager, I began to comprehend that my identity, character, attitudes, and actions were under the control of my personal choices. I understand the principle that the person I am today is the result of my choices yesterday. The person I'll be tomorrow will be the result of my choices today. Recognizing my ability to take responsibility for my thoughts and control them has been revolutionary.

The moment is clearly etched in my memory. I had just finished Bible School. I'd been experiencing stressful relationship conflicts—partly because of my immaturity and arrogance, I must admit! Attempts to change my attitudes seemed to fail. Although I earnestly loved God and was committed to His service, I permitted myself to become greatly discouraged, giving in to self-pity. I was sure I was worthless, useless, and hopeless. I was sinking into a state of depression.

However, that was about to change! One evening, I was sitting in a church service. The visiting minister simply but clearly showed from the Word of God how we let our minds be manipulated by destructive thoughts. Then he told us how we could make the choice to take back control of our thinking. In an instant, the lights turned on in my head!

My thoughts—positive or negative—are my responsibility. Although I understand this life-changing principle, it remains a daily choice to apply it. I choose to refuse to lose!

Purposeful Responsibility

In modern culture, our sense of personal responsibility often seems to be nonexistent. It has become normal to blame society in general, and others in particular, for the results of *our* decisions. Attempts are made to obscure the fact that every choice produces consequences.

In some schools, efforts have been made to make it impossible to get a failing grade. It is hoped this will make all students feel comfortable, whether they've done any work or not! The result, of course, is a sense of entitlement—everything is demanded and expected without effort. Albert

Schweitzer said, "Man must cease attributing his problems to his environment and learn again to exercise his will—his personal responsibility."[8]

> It is a good habit to often say to yourself, "I am responsible for my thoughts."

Responsibility involves being accountable for our decisions. It includes recognizing our own shortcomings and being willing to change. It embraces trustworthiness and dependability. Responsibility is constantly aware of consequences. It is a good habit to often say to yourself, "I am responsible for my thoughts."

Ralph Waldo Emerson is credited with writing, "Sow a thought and you reap an action; sow an act and you reap a habit; sow a habit and you reap a character; sow a character and you reap a destiny."[9] All the harvests of our choices will be the result of the seeds we plant in our minds today.

If we plant and cultivate corn, what do we expect to grow? The principle is the same: negative thinking has harmful and damaging outcomes; wholesome thoughts result in an optimistic and constructive harvest.

We cannot change the past. We cannot change others. We may not be able to change our circumstances. But we can *always* choose to change the way we think. Thoughts become part of our character as we meditate on them. We need to carefully choose the thoughts we permit to take root in our minds.

Passing the Blame

There are those who prefer to blame circumstances or other people for difficulties they experience. They try to deny or escape from taking responsibility for their thoughts or actions.

Society has aided abdication of responsibility by suggesting that some lifestyles and destructive habits are the result of sickness. What a treacherous, hopeless suggestion! The excuse then is, "I can't help myself. I'm sick."

We endeavor to pass the blame because we don't want to admit our behaviors are the direct result of the way we have chosen to think. We permit ourselves to be trapped in a place from which we can never be liberated. We are, in effect, saying, "I cannot help how I think. Everyone and everything around me is to blame for the person I have become."

Placing the blame on others or our circumstances only serves to entangle us more deeply in self-deception and hopelessness. This type of thinking prevents us from ever truly resolving our issues. We

We can never be free from those situations for which we refuse to take responsibility.

can never be free from those situations for which we refuse to take responsibility. The moment we become personally accountable for our thoughts and resulting behavior, we are on the road to liberation and transformation.

I heard of a woman who was going shopping. Her husband firmly told her not to buy a new dress. When she returned, however, she had a new dress. Her husband blew a gasket. He exclaimed, "I *told* you not to buy a dress!"

She confessed that was true, but admitted that the devil had tempted her. He countered, "You should have said, 'Get thee behind me, Satan.'"

"I did!" she retorted, "but then the devil told me, 'It looks good from back here too!'"

Passing the blame is an old game that started in the Garden of Eden. When Adam and Eve sinned, he blamed her and she blamed the serpent—and the serpent didn't have a leg to stand on!

One of the clearest signs of irresponsibility is when we make excuses for our thoughts and behaviors. Blaming someone else entangles us in webs of deceit and guilt. Taking responsibility, however, brings self-empowerment and freedom.

You are the king or queen in the castle of your own mind. Only you can determine the thoughts you permit to rule. This kingdom is uniquely yours. You are the only key holder.

Practicing Control

You are the master of your own thinking—the only person who decides what you think is you. Your opinions, beliefs, ideas, and deliberations are uniquely under your power.

We must take care of what we allow into our minds. Proverbs 4:23 states, *"Above all else, guard your heart, for it is the wellspring of life."* Our choice of thoughts determines if our lives will produce darkness or light, positive or negative impact, life or death. It's imperative for us to guard our hearts by protecting, defending, and shielding our minds from destructive external influences or from negative internal musings.

Someone illustrated our responsibility this way: "I cannot help it when birds fly over my head, but when they begin to build a nest in my hair I can do something about it."

I was once invited to join friends and other tourists to visit a castle. As we were walking across the grounds, I saw a pigeon score a bull's eye—making a large dump on the head of a bald man nearby. As his wife frantically used a handkerchief to wipe the excrement off his head, I began to giggle.

Entering the next building, I asked my friend if she had seen the episode. As we were laughing, I realized the man had come behind me and heard our chuckles at his expense. Rather dryly, he commented that we wouldn't find it so funny if it had happened to us. Without thinking, I quickly replied, "But sir, aren't you glad cows don't fly!"

We must decide which thoughts we will permit…

The point is, we can refuse to permit unwholesome thoughts from staying in our heads. We are continually bombarded by the media, circumstances, and human relationships. We may not be able to stop quick flashes of anger, lust, jealousy, bitterness, or fear. Our senses are exposed to a multitude of influences, like birds flying overhead. However, we can choose what will stay and what must go. And we must do it immediately.

There are multiple opportunities to permit anxious or angry thoughts to occupy our consciousness. Past misunderstandings and future uncertainties bring their baggage—piling up headaches and heartbreaks. We must decide which thoughts we permit and how deeply we let them take root.

We cannot spend our time watching sordid affairs on television or listening to dishonest and corrupt conversations and keep a carefree, Holy-Spirit-controlled mind. We cannot fill our eyes and ears with perversion and filthy language without it affecting us. It will produce unwholesome fantasies, discontentment, guilt, and shame. It will waste our time, steal our relationships, and sap our energy.

We must set a watch over our minds. Psalm 19:14 encourages us to take this responsibility: *"May the words of my mouth and the meditation of my heart be pleasing in your sight, O Lord, my Rock and my Redeemer."* We must not evade our responsibilities. We can determine to turn off our televisions or internet. We can choose to throw out trashy magazines. We can decide to fill our hearts and homes with positive and uplifting atmospheres. It is our responsibility to discipline our own minds. No one else, not even the Lord, can make these choices for us.

Questions to Assist Practical Application

1. How would you define responsibility? Have you recognized the importance of personal responsibility for your thoughts?

2. What are some consequences you have experienced because of your choice of thoughts?

3. What is the result of passing the blame? Have you been trying to evade or make excuses for your thoughts and behaviors?

4. Can you identify areas in which you need to take responsibility for your thoughts?

5. What sources do you permit to influence the way you think?

6. Can you name people who have influenced you by their positive manner of life?

Challenge
*"The mind of sinful man is death,
but the mind controlled by the Spirit
is life and peace."*
Romans 8:6

chapter three

Relying on Spiritual Resources

*Love the Lord your God with all your heart
and with all your soul and with all your mind.*
Matthew 22:37

*You will keep in perfect peace him whose mind is
steadfast, because he trusts in you.*
Isaiah 26:3

There is power in positive thinking. Positive thoughts produce healthier and happier brains. It is scientific fact that bright, optimistic, and uplifting input can actually change brain function. Dr. Caroline Leaf, a leading brain scientist, refers to the new field of science known as epigenetics. Human genetic composition can literally be changed by the way we think.[10]

However, there is a dimension which far supersedes merely thinking positive thoughts. It is the revolution of

Holy-Spirit-controlled thinking. When we submit our thoughts to the Spirit of God and the Word of God, He transforms the deepest part of our beings. Jesus spoke of being born again—or, literally translated, being born from above (John 3:3).

> *When heart conversion happens, we experience radical change from the inside out.*

Positive thinking alone can *never* produce a converted heart or peace with God. When heart conversion happens, we experience radical change from the inside out.

This begins with the recognition and conviction of our sinfulness. We are troubled by the darkness of our hearts. We are awakened to our need of forgiveness from God and of relationship with Him. We are deeply concerned for our spiritual condition as we are confronted with the fact of our guilt before God.

We may try to change our external identity—try to be a better person—but there is no escape from the guilt of the past. The situation is similar to credit card debt. We can decide to never use the card again, but we must still deal with the debt.

The Bible teaches that Jesus Christ, the perfect and sinless Son of God, came to pay the penalty for our sin so we could be restored in relationship with God. When we repent of our sin, we experience a *change of mind* toward our sin. We turn from the ways of darkness and evil, surrendering to the Lordship of Jesus who died for us.

When we repent, His power releases us from the guilt of sin. We experience His personal presence, bringing peace and transformation. He sets our lives on a new path in which we want to please Him by doing what is right. This is described in 2 Corinthians 5:17: *"Therefore if any man be in Christ, he is a new creature: old things are passed away; behold, all things are become new"* (KJV).

His Word teaches us the principles of how a follower of Jesus should live. It becomes our desire to show others the beauty of God's love. The Lord empowers us to walk with Him.

We read in Romans 12:1–2,

And so, dear brothers and sisters, I plead with you to give your bodies to God. Let them be a living and holy sacrifice—the kind he will accept. When you think of what he has done for you, is this too much to ask? Don't copy the behavior and customs of this world, but let God transform you into a new person by changing the way you think. Then you will know what God wants you to do, and you will know how good and pleasing and perfect his will really is. (NLT)

Christ will begin to be reflected in your attitudes, words, and actions as you let God transform you into a new person by changing the way you think. The Holy Spirit begins His great work of regenerating your values, renewing your priorities, and reeducating your conscience.

The Bible tells us, however, that we have a lethal spiritual enemy who utilizes his entire arsenal to bring destruction and darkness into our lives. We are admonished to use the armor of God to withstand him. In Ephesians 6:16, we are told, *"In addition to all this, take up the shield of faith, with which you can extinguish all the flaming arrows of the evil one."*

Satan uses temptation, deception, and accusation to accomplish his dirty work. We are tempted through the appetites of our senses. Satan insists we have the right to instant gratification. Deception causes us to believe twisted truth. His purpose is to blind our hearts, preventing us from trusting and obeying Jesus Christ and from believing His Word. It is, however, his accusations which can wreak havoc in our minds.

After shooting his arrows of evil thoughts at us, he stands as the accuser, telling us how wicked we are. But *he* was the author of those thoughts! No wonder he's called the father of lies (John 8:44).

We must be vigilant to recognize his tricks. We can stand guard to protect our minds by refusing to let his dark thoughts gain a foothold in our meditation. There are four ways by which we can instantly know if God or Satan is the source of our thoughts:

- God always speaks through the conscience. Satan always speaks through the reasoning of the mind, offering excuses and urging us to avoid responsibility for our behavior.
- God always speaks light, love, hope, and peace—with the opportunity for repentance and change. Satan always brings darkness, fear, hopelessness, and guilt—with no possibility of redemption.
- When God speaks, He always addresses specific issues, convicting and defining personal sin. Satan always brings a vague cloud of darkness, leaving us uneasy and unsure of the root problem.
- When God speaks, He always offers forgiveness in response to repentance. We have the eternal promise of 1 John 1:9—*"If we confess our sins, he is faithful*

and just and will forgive us our sins and purify us from all unrighteousness." Satan, however, never releases or forgives but torments the mind with despair and fear.

The Holy Spirit has provided spiritual resources to aid us against these unseen forces. He doesn't leave us alone in this battle but comes alongside us with powerful and effective weapons. The study of the Word of God and prayer in the name of Jesus are basic equipment for every believer. There is power in the blood of Jesus to destroy strongholds of habitual thinking. Turning our hearts to God with praise and thanksgiving releases peace and joy.

The Protection of the Word of God

The Word of God is an effective weapon which can be used to change the way we think. The promises and principles of His Word are like a spiritual sword bringing victory in every conflict (Ephesians 6:17). Memorize and utilize the Word of God. When Jesus was tempted by Satan, He used the Word of God to overcome. In response to every demonic temptation, Jesus replied, *"It is written"* (Luke 4:4, 8, 12).

We read in 2 Corinthians 10:4–5,

(For the weapons of our warfare are not carnal, but mighty through God to the pulling down of strong holds;) Casting down imaginations, and every high thing that exalteth itself against the knowledge of God, and bringing into captivity every thought to the obedience of Christ. (KJV)

There is power as we meditate on God's Word and speak its promises against destructive thought patterns. The Word of God provides us with the response to arguments and human reasoning. By using the authority of His Word, thoughts can be seized and subjected to the control of Christ.

By using the authority of His Word, thoughts can be seized and subjected to the control of Christ.

Sometimes difficulties in my life produce thoughts of discouragement. During those times, I have been amazed as the Lord brought to my heart wonderful, effective, and practical promises from His Word. Verses from the Bible suddenly became alive, giving me solutions and courage. The Word of God is a vital, living book with relevant answers to daily situations.

Knowledge of the Scriptures, and applying them to our lives on a daily basis, will protect us from deception: *"Do not merely listen to the word, and so deceive yourselves. Do what it says"* (James 1:22). We will be guided by understanding spiritual principles and instruction in truth. I once saw these words written on the flyleaf of a Bible: "This book will keep you from sin and sin will keep you from this book."

Reading the Bible, memorizing verses, and studying its principles and promises are excellent ways to fill our thoughts with hope and courage. When our minds are filled with the truth and light found in God's Word, there is little room left for darkness and selfishness.

The Power of the Name of Jesus

Prayer in the name of Jesus is a spiritual weapon. Many examples help us understand the authority available when we use the name of Jesus. For instance, a policeman can raise his hand and make an eighteen-wheeler come to a screeching halt. In his own strength, he cannot force the truck to stop. However, when he stands in his uniform, he has all the authority of his government and nation behind him.

We couldn't hope to conquer many habitual thought patterns by our own strength, but when we stand in the name of Jesus, all the authority of heaven stands with us.

The Bible says in Philippians 2:9–11,

> *Therefore God exalted him to the highest place and gave him the name that is above every name, that at the name of Jesus every knee should bow, in heaven and on earth and under the earth, and every tongue confess that Jesus Christ is Lord, to the glory of God the Father.*

We don't use the name of Jesus as a magic word. When we submit to Jesus as our Lord and Savior, our purpose is to please Him. By using His name in prayer, we find grace to live for Christ. We no longer live for our own pleasure but that His love will be manifested through us.

> *Satan cannot stand before the powerful, conquering name of Jesus.*

Satan cannot stand before the powerful, conquering name of Jesus. It is written in Luke 10:19, *"I have given you authority… to overcome all the power of the enemy."*

We can bring our downhearted thoughts and discouragements to God in prayer. The comforting words of the old familiar hymn "What a Friend We Have in Jesus," written by Joseph M. Scriven, say it well:

What a friend we have in Jesus, all our sins and griefs to bear!
What a privilege to carry everything to God in prayer!
Oh, what peace we often forfeit, oh, what needless pain we bear,
All because we do not carry everything to God in prayer![11]

In the name of Jesus, we can present our requests to God and expect Him to work on our behalf. We have the marvelous promise of Hebrews 4:16, which says, *"Let us then approach the throne of grace with confidence, so that we may receive mercy and find grace to help us in our time of need."*

The Potency of the Blood of Jesus

The blood of Jesus provides a unique spiritual weapon. Why do we speak about the power of the blood of Jesus? The Bible teaches that the life of the flesh is in the blood:

> *For the life of a creature is in the blood, and I have given it to you to make atonement for yourselves on the altar; it is the blood that makes atonement for one's life.* (Leviticus 17:11)

Therefore, the blood of Jesus represents the *life* of the Son of God.

God had a will for mankind, but His testament could never be released until the blood (life) of the Son of God was poured out. Only after death can the will of the testator come into effect. This is what the Bible teaches in Hebrews 9:16–17:

In the case of a will, it is necessary to prove the death of the one who made it, because a will is in force only when somebody has died; it never takes effect while the one who made it is living.

When Jesus died on the cross and His blood was shed, it released the will (the New Testament) of God. All the promises of God provided in the New Testament are available for us because of the blood Jesus shed.

In Revelation 12:10–11, it is written,

For the accuser of our brothers, who accuses them before our God day and night, has been hurled down. They overcame him by the blood of the Lamb and by the word of their testimony.

Choose A Changed Mind

You may ask, "How can the blood of Jesus be used as a spiritual weapon to change the way I think?" Let me use this example. Suppose whenever you see a certain person or reflect on a hurtful situation, your mind jumps into the same old track, reviewing your troubling circumstances. Even when you determine to pray for that person, you relive the pain. Your prayer degenerates into a rehearsal of the ugly details and what you would like to say to that person if you ever get the chance.

That thought pattern has become a stronghold in your mind. How can it be destroyed and transformed? By taking the whole situation, including your attitudes, to the cross of Christ and submitting it to the power of the blood of Jesus.

If your wrists were tied and someone poured acid on the rope, what would happen? Depending on the strength of the acid and the frequency of application, the acid would eventually eat through the rope. By the same principle, you can dip the brush of your will into the blood of Jesus and paint it over destructive and painful thought patterns.

Every time you think those bitter, unforgiving thoughts, paint them with the blood of Jesus. It might take a few days, weeks, or months, but sooner or later the blood of Jesus will destroy the bitterness and heal the pain. The transformation will be accomplished depending on the frequency and strength of faith with which you apply the blood of Jesus.

The Privilege of Praise and Thanksgiving

Thanksgiving and praise to God breaks heavy chains, flooding our minds with peace and joy. The Apostle Paul encouraged the principle of thanksgiving in 1 Thessalonians 5:18, telling us to *"give thanks in all circumstances, for this is God's will for you in Christ Jesus."*

Expressing gratitude is a powerful key to changing the way we think. It is impossible to be discouraged, depressed, or unhappy if we choose to let true thankfulness rise up within us. As we focus on the blessings and benefits that come our way, an attitude of gratitude will replace our doldrums with cheerful song. We can continually reflect and review the blessings of life.

It is a good exercise to literally count our blessings. We can write down all the wonderful experiences, provisions, and friendships we enjoy. It doesn't take long before we realize how much we have for which to be thankful.

We can make it a habit to give thanks. Thankful thinking is a choice. Even if we don't feel like it, we can make the effort to express

Thankful thinking is a choice.

gratefulness in every situation and to everyone we meet. It is surprising how gratitude can spread—transforming heaviness in the atmosphere, releasing joy within our own minds, and refreshing others.

An elderly acquaintance of mine had settled into the habit of complaint. No matter what good was done for her, she always found something to grumble about. She was unhappy, malcontented, and critical. I challenged her to begin to express thankfulness. When she did, her whole demeanor changed.

The Bible is filled with praises to God. We can chase away darkness by simply speaking words of praise and thanksgiving to the Lord. It is a wonderful, refreshing habit to speak or sing our expressions of gratefulness to Him out loud.

Cicero wrote, "A thankful heart is not only the greatest virtue, but the parent of all the other virtues."[12]

A little poem by an unknown author says it well:

Thank God for dirty dishes;
They have a tale to tell.
While others may go hungry,
We're eating very well.
With home, health, and happiness,

I shouldn't want to fuss;
By the stack of evidence,
God's been very good to us.[13]

During a conversation, a friend of mine commented,
- We can be thankful for a leaky roof and dirty floors because it means we have a home.
- We can be thankful for dirty clothes because it means we have clothes to wear and washing machines to clean them.
- We can be thankful for parking spaces far from the shopping mall entrance because we have legs to walk and money to spend.

Although God has given us weapons to defeat darkness and the spiritual forces that attack our minds, they will only be effective if we use them.

In his book, *Everyone Communicates, Few Connect*, John Maxwell retells Norm Lawson's story:

A rabbi and a soap maker went for a walk together. The soap maker said, "What good is religion? Look at all the trouble and misery of the world! Still there, even after years—thousands of years—of teaching about goodness and truth and peace. Still there, after all the prayers and sermons and teachings. If religion is good and true, why should this be?"

The rabbi said nothing. They continued walking until he noticed a child playing in the gutter.

Then the rabbi said, "Look at that child. You say that soap makes people clean, but see the dirt on that youngster. Of what good is soap? With all the soap in the world, over all these years, the child is still filthy. I wonder how effective soap is, after all!"

The soap maker protested, "But, Rabbi, soap cannot do any good unless it is used!"

"Exactly," replied the rabbi.[14]

We can experience supernatural help in the battle to bring our minds under control. The spiritual weapons of the Word of God, the name of Jesus, and the blood of Jesus can effectively destroy strongholds of habitual thoughts. Praising God brings new perspective, assurance, and vitality to our minds.

Questions to Assist Practical Application

1. Have you surrendered your life to Jesus Christ? If not, why not do it now?

2. Have you recognized Satan's attempts to influence your thoughts? Have you recognized God's voice filled with love and hope?

3. Is the study of God's Word a priority in your life? Do you consider prayer in the name of Jesus to be a vital source of spiritual strength?

4. Are you willing to address destructive strongholds in your mind? Will you apply the blood of Jesus by faith to those habitual thought patterns?

5. Are your thoughts filled with gratefulness? In what ways could you more effectively express gratitude to God and others?

Challenge

*"You, dear children, are from God
and have overcome them,
because the one who is in you is greater
than the one who is in the world."*

1 John 4:4

chapter four
Refusing Poisonous Thoughts

The happiness of your life depends upon the quality
of your thoughts:
therefore, guard accordingly,
and take care that you entertain
no notions unsuitable to virtue
and reasonable nature.
Marcus Aurelius[15]

Anger will never disappear so long as thoughts of
resentment are cherished in the mind.
Anger will disappear just as soon as
thoughts of resentment are forgotten.
John Dryden[16]

As sovereign rulers over our minds, we choose what we think. We have the authority to permit or forbid thoughts from lodging in our minds. We need to arrest unproductive and unhealthy meditations. Some ideas need to be met with a broom at the door! Don't even entertain them. Give them the boot!

> *Selfishness nourishes toxins of the mind.*

David, the psalmist, included these words in Psalm 139:2: *"thou understandest my thought afar off"* (KJV). It's comforting to know God understands our thoughts. Sometimes our brains seem overloaded with data, jumbled with confusion. We cannot understand our own reasoning. Nevertheless, it remains our personal obligation to collect our thoughts, bring order to our inner world, and determine proper reactions.

Selfishness nourishes toxins of the mind. The desire to comfort, protect, and gratify our egos can seem to be legitimate. Unfortunately, this egocentricity usually results in fear-filled, angry, self-indulgent thoughts.

If we give ourselves permission, our minds can reopen wounds, relive conflicts, and rehash ugly details of past hurts. As a result, we desire to run in fear, seethe with anger, or collapse in tears. These reactions are rooted in lethal, poisonous thoughts.

The Poison of Fear-Filled Thinking

Instinctive fears can be linked with self-preservation. There are also abnormal, irrational phobias. Some fears are related to our lack of acceptance, others to our perceived imperfections or failures, while still others are based on difficult past experiences or concern for the future. Whatever the source of our fears, they always have a negative impact on our lives.

Much fear involves the apprehension of rejection and our desire to be accepted. It has been observed that at age twenty, we worry about what others think of us. At forty, we don't care what they think. At sixty, we realize they haven't been thinking of us at all!

A young person may be sensitive about his appearance and desire to be accepted by others of the same age. Afraid to be different, he follows the fads, hoping for approval. Meanwhile, those he's trying to impress are likewise terrified of rejection! The result is a group of young people all secretly scared stiff of what others are thinking. This compulsion to conform, to belong, and to be accepted is the natural human desire for love, hijacked by fear. We call it peer pressure.

Comparing ourselves with one another also feeds unnecessary anguish. Fear of failure and feelings of inadequacy fill us with apprehension, even dread. Our perception of our inabilities can leave us incapable of progress.

A very dear friend of mine is one of the most talented, intelligent, and capable young women I know. However, when she was younger, much of her tremendous skill was paralyzed by her fear of failure and of what others thought of her. She would agonize over details, deeply concerned she would make some mistake. She was terrified of public appearances for fear others wouldn't like her. If some effort turned out badly, she berated herself, convinced she was hopeless, stupid, and could never succeed.

Slowly she began to understand that her fears were baseless. It was a long, sometimes painful process. With much encouragement, she began to break free from the senseless torment. Positive encouragement was poured into her. On one occasion, a particular statement of faith was spoken to her. In answer to prayer and with conscious change of thought patterns, she experienced transformation. She has become a beautiful, confident, and effective leader who touches hundreds of lives.

> *Stress can be caused by living our lives in contradiction to our core values.*

Stress, likewise, is related to fear. Stress can be caused by living our lives in contradiction to our core values. The strain of balancing who we *are* and what we are *doing* creates inner pressure. The external hassle is only the tip of the iceberg. The hidden tension and angst gnaws at the heart, slowly destroying one's mind and body.

Fear is the root of anxiety and worry. Someone said that ninety-eight percent of the things we worry about will never happen, and the two percent that do happen never take place the way we envisioned!

We become deeply concerned about the necessities of life. How will we survive? How will these issues be resolved? What will happen tomorrow? The Word of God instructs us in Philippians 4:6–7,

> *Do not be anxious about anything, but in everything, by prayer and petition, with thanksgiving, present your requests to God. And the peace of God, which transcends all understanding, will guard your hearts and your minds in Christ Jesus.*

This passage reminds us that we can take all our issues to God in prayer. Sometimes our worries can be clarified and resolved by simply identifying them verbally. Certainly trusting in the faithfulness of the Lord soothes the fretful soul.

There is a choice involved in *not letting* our hearts be troubled. We can choose the wonderful promise Jesus left His disciples in John 14:27:

Peace I leave with you; my peace I give you. I do not give to you as the world gives. Do not let your hearts be troubled and do not be afraid.

Perhaps because I'm a natural organizer and like to have plans laid out clearly in advance, anxious thoughts can pour into my head. I've learned from experience that I must refuse to dwell on concerns that produce anxiety. I must handle the necessary details, then fill my mind with the positive promises of God's Word. (I'm a "work in progress," but improvement is happening!)

Don't waste time thinking about the past or the future. Neither produces any solutions. Learn to live in the now. Jesus said in Matthew 6:25,

Therefore I tell you, do not worry about your life, what you will eat or drink; or about your body, what you will wear. Is not life more important than food, and the body more important than clothes?

Dr. Caroline Leaf made the interesting observation that all emotions can be placed in one of two categories. On the negative side, everything can be summed up by fear. By contrast, every positive thought is rooted in love.[17] Remarkably, this is exactly what the Bible teaches. John wrote in 1 John 4:18, *"There is no fear in love. But perfect love drives out fear, because fear has to do with punishment. The one who fears is not made perfect in love."*

We don't have to be tormented by fear. When we experience peace with God through Jesus Christ, our hearts are filled with His love. We can permit His presence and peace to fill our minds. In Colossians 3:15, it is written, *"Let the peace of Christ rule in your hearts…"* We can choose to let peace rule our thoughts.

The Poison of Anger-Filled Thinking

Anger is also related to fear. It exerts tremendously destructive and negative influences in our brains, as well as on our health. Anger is selfish and demanding, often consuming our thoughts when people don't meet our needs.

Anger rooted in unrealistic expectations of oneself or others can lead to discouragement and depression. Frustration can grow when we aren't able to achieve the progress we desire. If we let it, irritation will smolder, gradually building within us. Bitterness and resentment can cause stress and burnout. Other people's words and actions can result in deep pain. If we choose to meditate on past hurts, they'll escalate into festering wounds. Someone once described bitterness as drinking poison and hoping your enemy will be the one to die!

> *The most powerful antidote for anger is forgiveness.*

The most powerful antidote for anger is forgiveness. You can choose to forgive. You can make a conscious choice to let forgiving thoughts take the place of anger. Tension and bitterness will dissipate. It has been said that when you forgive someone, you set a prisoner free and discover it was you all along.

Forgiveness is basically the decision to let go of our rights for revenge. It's our choice to stop demanding punishment for perceived offences. Forgiveness is the willingness to stop carrying resentment and anger. Forgiveness doesn't imply approval for the wrongs done. Neither is it the same as trust, which must be earned and is built on future relationship.

A four-year-old girl once learned to recite the Lord's Prayer. Although she had misunderstood the proper words, her prayer was genuine: "Forgive us our trash baskets as we forgive those who put trash in our baskets."

> We have the right not to be offended.

Forgiveness is simply letting go of grudges and bitterness—with no strings attached. We can make the choice to forgive those who do us wrong. We have the right *not* to be offended. In Colossians 3:13, we are admonished, *"Bear with each other and forgive whatever grievances you may have against one another. Forgive as the Lord forgave you."*

Don't dwell on all the bitter experiences of life. Forgive and forget. When you receive the Lord's abundant forgiveness, surely you can offer the same to others. Don't rehash the past. Even a cat knows some things need to be buried! This is the time to move past the anger poisoning your mind. Release forgiveness. Receive freedom.

The Poison of Self-Centered Thinking

We need to refuse to entertain self-centered thinking. Too much introspection isn't healthy. Yes, the Bible tells us to examine ourselves. There are moments when we need to look carefully into our own hearts. If there is evil, rebellion, or wrong motives in our hearts, we need to confess our sins to God and thoroughly repent by turning away from them. Then we must trust in God's faithful forgiveness and continue on our way.

Unfortunately, some people constantly dig up their sins, past failures, and mistakes. When we confess and forsake our sins, God promises to cast them into the sea of His forgetfulness (Psalm 103:12). Then He puts up a sign saying, "Don't fish here!"

Refuse to spend your days looking within, trying to remember all your mistakes. If God convicts you of something specific, hold it up to the light of God's Word and His promises. Let the light expose it and the blood of Jesus destroy it. Then get on with life.

Once, when Jesus was casting out devils, the Pharisees accused Him of casting out demon spirits by the prince of the devils, known to them as Beelzebub. The word Beelzebub is derived from the title "God of the flies"—or literally, "God of manure." It was thought that flies were produced by spontaneous regeneration in manure. This name is a very good description of Satan and his evil forces.

It's amazing how quickly flies arrive on a dead or decaying carcass. Why? Because they, like the devil, are attracted to decay. There is danger in indulging in perverted and self-centered thinking, because it produces decay in the mind and heart.

Some depression is caused by chemical imbalance and mental illness. However, it's often a result of bitterness and unforgiveness, multiplied by self-pity. Some people can pinpoint the exact moment their depression began. Perhaps it started with divorce papers or the death of a spouse. Maybe conflict or the loss of a job created a precipitating crisis. They experience fear, anger, and frustration and become self-absorbed in the problem. Their victim mentality is fed by the sense that everyone and everything is against them. Gradually, their self-pity descends into despair. This, in turn, can lead to depression.

Those who become deeply despondent sink into a pit of egocentric thought. They become incapable of looking beyond themselves. Depressed people may find it hard to worship God because it becomes increasingly difficult for them to think of anything outside themselves.

> *...loneliness is really habitual thoughts of feeling sorry for oneself!*

Self-pity wears many acceptable disguises. For example, one will often speak of how difficult life is because of loneliness. However, further investigation reveals that loneliness is really habitual thoughts of feeling sorry for oneself! They think, "No one loves me. No one has time for me. No one really cares about me." The key word here is *me*.

A very dear friend found herself quite alone one weekend. The office was closed and most of her close friends were out of town. Her sense of isolation began to overtake her. Feeling forlorn and lonesome, she remembered that I had defined loneliness as a disguise for self-pity. Laughing, she confided to me later, "Suddenly feeling lonely didn't seem nearly so romantic!"

We also find self-pity hidden under the socially acceptable catchphrase of "poor self-esteem." Low self-image is often used as an excuse to explain why some people never escape from cycles of failure. In reality, they often do not succeed because it has become their habit of thinking they will never succeed. Some people make a fetish of their failures. They compare themselves to others and allow thoughts of inferiority to control, even paralyze, their minds. Most self-image problems are directly related to one's refusal to take responsibility for personal choices.

> *We can refuse to be victims.*

If we would expose self-pity and reveal it for the self-centered thinking it is, perhaps we would be better equipped to avoid its destructive power. We too easily use loneliness and poor self-esteem as excuses to nurse victim mentalities. We can refuse to be victims.

How do you refuse to have a victim mentality? Reject undisciplined thinking. Meet those thoughts at the door of your mind and deny them entrance. Choose to seek solutions for your problems instead of justification for failures.

We are responsible to protect our minds by rejecting toxic, destructive thoughts. We must refuse fear-filled, anxious thoughts. We must decide to destroy the roots of anger by releasing forgiveness and mercy. We must no longer cling to excuses for self-pity or self-centeredness. We can replace harmful thoughts with life-giving and enriching inspirations.

Questions to Assist Practical Application

1. Is your mind tormented by fear-filled thoughts? How are you influenced by peer pressure? What are you most anxious about?

2. Do you recognize the thought patterns that cause your anger? Are you willing to give and receive forgiveness?

3. To relieve stress, what changes can you make in the way you think?

4. Does self-centeredness or self-pity determine your mindset? Can you remember moments when you refused a victim mentality?

5. Do you recognize your responsibility and ability to discipline your own thoughts?

Challenge
"Search me, O God, and know my heart;
test me and know my anxious thoughts."
Psalm 139:23

chapter five
Renewing Thought Patterns

The secret of living a life of excellence
is merely a matter of thinking thoughts of excellence.
Really, it's a matter of programming our minds
with the kind of information that will set us free.
Charles R. Swindoll[18]

It takes but one positive thought when given
a chance to survive and thrive
to overpower an entire army of negative thoughts.
Robert H Schuller[19]

On a beautiful summer day with bright sunshine, I was working in the garden. But my thoughts were troubled. An acquaintance with a thorny personality had said aggravating words to me a couple of hours before. As I turned the conversation around in my mind, I felt more and more irritated with the person. I was holding little conversations in my head—what he had said and what I would have liked to say back to him! I became more and more annoyed. The angrier I became, the harder I hoed. The whole situation ticked me off!

> *We can choose to fill our minds with positive, productive thoughts by replacing bad thoughts with good thoughts.*

A movement caught my eye. I turned suddenly... and nearly fainted with fright! My fright quickly turned to astonishment, then fascination and thrill. Three incredibly cute young skunk kits had appeared from nowhere and were walking deliberately in a straight line across my garden scarcely a meter from me, their little tails waving warning flags behind them. I didn't dare breathe—for more reasons than one!

Excitedly, I screeched to my neighbor, who was working in her garden next door. Together we gaped in amazement as they wandered off into the bushes. Where they came from, where their mother was, or where they were going was anyone's guess. In one split second, however, all my annoyance and irritation vanished!

This illustrates a practical way to help us change the way we think—the principle of replacement. We can only hold a limited number of ideas in our conscious minds at one time, so if we're occupied with uplifting, life-giving thoughts, there's simply no room for evil. We can choose to fill our minds with positive, productive thoughts by *replacing* bad thoughts with good thoughts.

Light and darkness cannot coexist. Light always conquers darkness. When we choose to fill our minds with quality values, darkness vanishes. Minds flooded with light have no room for gloom. The Apostle Paul gave us a list of profitable thoughts. In Philippians 4:8, he declared,

Finally, brothers, whatever is true, whatever is noble, whatever is right, whatever is pure, whatever is lovely, whatever is admirable—if anything is excellent or praiseworthy—think about such things.

Each of the eight categories listed in this scripture contains profound, mind-changing principles. Let's take the challenge—chuck the garbage out of our heads and replace it with these values.

Thinking What Is True

Think about what is true. Our thoughts need to be based on real experience, the reality of what's actually happening. On one occasion while travelling on a long, difficult road, fear-filled thoughts gripped my imagination. I felt paralyzed as I reflected about all the horrible incidents that could happen to me. What if I had car trouble? What if I became ill? What if I was attacked? What would I do? What if, what if? Terror seized me.

A friend prayed with me. Later, I read a sentence that defined my situation: "God doesn't give us grace for our imagination, but for our experience." The imaginations weren't real experiences. At that moment, I didn't have any problems—only imaginations prefixed with *what ifs*. When I would pass through *real* crises, the grace of God would be more than enough to sustain me.

> We often jump to untrue conclusions and make false assumptions...

We often jump to untrue conclusions and make false assumptions about others, about God, about church, about ourselves, or about our future. We spend hours being upset, ticked-off, anxious, and fearful about things that simply aren't true, but which we have *assumed* to be fact.

I have a wonderful brother-in-law. In fact, he's on my list of most admired men. However, nobody on the planet can get under my skin quite so well as he can—because there can only be so many perfect people in one place at one time! On a number of occasions, he and I have bumped halos during rather intense dialogs.

After one such discussion, I was particularly annoyed. A few moments later, as I was standing in a large crowd, I noticed him across the room talking to his son. As I glanced their way, they both began laughing—then they both turned and looked at me.

I immediately jumped to the conclusion that not only was he getting his jollies laughing at me, but he was including my nephew in the joke as well. My blood pressure went straight up. It was enough to give me a hot flash! I was quite offended.

Several months passed before I had an opportunity to confront him. My wounds were deep and my offence strong. Finally, with my sister as mediator, I found the occasion to inform him of my wounded pride! "Like the time I saw you and my nephew laughing at me!" I chided him, reminding him of the incident.

His eyes grew round as dinner plates. Astonished, he informed me they hadn't been laughing at me at all. He then explained his side of the story. Talk about a paradigm shift! The wind went right out of my sails. It was my turn to be astonished. I had jumped to a false conclusion. I had been carrying anger and hurt over an imagined offence for weeks. I had been ticked-off about something that wasn't even true.

At the end of the episode, my sister made the sage observation, "We must learn to always think the very best about people and circumstances until the worst is proven, and even then always think the best option possible."

Thinking What Is Noble

Seeking to think the best about other people—or our own circumstances—is an excellent definition of what it means to nurture noble thoughts. This has also been translated as "honourable" thoughts (according to the American Standard Version of the Bible). This word conveys quality, grace, and dignity.

A number of years ago, I had an alarm installed on my car. I was intrigued by the manner in which the wiring was hidden. When I commented on it, I was amazed by the mechanic's response: "In order to install these crime deterrents, one must think like a criminal. We have to be able to see in advance how they'll seize their opportunity for crime. We have to reason with the criminal mind to have an advantage."

It is astounding that some people spend all their energy trying to beat the system by seeking crooked, harmful, and evil ways to achieve their ends. Imagine the good that could be achieved if they would use the strength of their intellect for honest and noble causes!

Honest thoughts must be rooted in true integrity. The root of the word integrity means whole and without mixture. When we have opportunities to think and do evil, we sense the conviction of the Holy Spirit within our conscience. Our reaction to the voice of God is the measure of our integrity. A tender conscience will quickly repent and seek forgiveness; lack of integrity will seek to excuse and hide evil.

Some may believe they can unleash uncontrolled thoughts in the secret corridors of their minds. Although they may sense guilt, they make excuse by suggesting that this is their private world. They resent the censorship of the conscience interfering in their personal meditations. True integrity, by contrast, exudes transparency of life and thought; there are no hidden skeletons in dark closets.

> *Honest thoughts must be rooted in true integrity.*

I had the opportunity to share some time with a pastor's wife. I knew she had passed through some very serious and painful situations because of others' cruel words and actions. I was amazed, however, by her consistent, honorable reference to those who had wronged her. I was astonished by the dignity and grace of the words she spoke, words which came from her choice to think the best of difficult people and situations.

Thinking What Is Just

Meditate on that which is *just*, or *right*. Justice (or fairness) is one of the basic principles of life. We claim our rights and shout "That's not fair!" to others who dare cross our sense of justice. Thinking just thoughts isn't about being critical of others, but rather contemplating how we can rightly live with supreme fairness to all.

There are those who bristle at being crossed, getting defensive over every injustice done to them. They continually guard the memories of past wrongs but don't appreciate being reminded of their own errors. We must choose a different path. We must be willing to take seriously our responsibility for perceived injustice and seek ways to bring peace and equality. These actions will only come from minds that concentrate on weighing situations fairly.

> We must seek just thoughts while guarding against judgmental attitudes.

Two young children were having a very noisy squabble.

One had a toy; the other wanted it. Their mother stepped in to referee. With a little reasoning and a warning, she succeeded in fair distribution, resolving the conflict. Her level head brought about a peaceful solution. We can apply the same principle to every battle.

We must seek just thoughts while guarding against judgmental attitudes. Jesus made this solemn declaration:

Do not judge, or you too will be judged. For in the same way you judge others, you will be judged, and with the measure you use, it will be measured to you. Why do you look at the speck of sawdust in your brother's eye and pay no attention to the plank in your own eye? How can you say to your brother, "Let me take the speck out of your eye," when all the time there is a plank in your own eye? You hypocrite, first take the plank out of your own eye, and then you will see clearly to remove the speck from your brother's eye. (Matthew 7:1–5)

On a newscast, I heard a local politician apologize for an apparent misuse of public funds. She took total responsibility, admitting it had been an oversight on her part. She expressed her desire to pay back what she owed. I was struck, however, by the intense criticism, not to mention accusations of insincerity, immediately hurled at her.

Time and actions will eventually prove if she is honest, but the biting remarks and disparaging denunciation were painful to listen to—spoken by some who didn't even know her!

How easy, but how *dangerous*, it is for us to judge people. Only God knows one's true motives. Each heart knows its own joy and sorrow. We must guard our minds and lips from condemning others and rather seek uncritical thoughts of justice.

Thinking What Is Pure

Purity of thought produces wholesome character. In comparison, those who have given their minds to impurity feed on perversion, innuendo, and crass humor. They are incapable of recognizing their depravity. The Bible declares in Titus 1:15, *"To the pure, all things are pure, but to those who are corrupted and do not believe, nothing is pure. In fact, both their minds and consciences are corrupted."*

There is something profoundly destructive about habitual, impure meditation. Entertaining lewd and lustful thoughts promises thrills and selfish gratification, but it eventually produces slavery to degradation and debauchery.

This downward spiral results in guilt, loneliness, and brokenness. There's never any real satisfaction, only the continual search for elusive happiness.

Pornography has become a billion-dollar business, but the broken homes, damaged consciences, and twisted values in its wake can never be measured. Beauty has been destroyed. Rottenness eats the mind and decays the soul.

Among the Beatitudes, we read in Matthew 5:8, *"Blessed are the pure in heart, for they will see God."* Purity of character begins with meditations of the heart. The continual cultivation of pure thought creates cleanness of conscience, as well as transparency of life. A pure mind doesn't lose vital energy to condemnation and guilt.

> Purity of character begins with meditations of the heart.

If we are disciplined in permitting only wholesome thoughts, they have a powerful ability to release peace and healing in our minds. Purity will be manifested in every aspect of our lives.

Thinking What Is Lovely

To think on what is lovely includes the appreciation of beauty—in creation, in character, in creativity, and in culture.

The magnificence of nature with all its diversity can fill us with wonder and reverence—the splendor of sunsets, the scent of blooming roses, the sounds of birdsong.

I have had opportunities to see many scenic attractions—a geyser in Iceland, the Alps of Switzerland, a tulip garden in Holland, a prairie sunrise. On occasion, the beauty of nature takes my breath away.

> *We recognize that our problems are insignificant in the light of His magnitude.*

A simple walk in the garden can refresh the mind. It takes us out of ourselves to see the greatness of God. We recognize that our problems are insignificant in the light of His magnitude.

It is very stimulating and refreshing to interact with people of rich character. Those who exude kindness, cheerfulness, and compassion bring such beauty to the lives of everyone they meet.

Several members of my family are very talented artists (an ability that totally passed me by). It is amazing to watch as they slap a few brush lines on a canvas. Suddenly, a gorgeous painting appears! Listening to skilled musicians can be breathtaking. I am inspired by the creative ability God has put in us. Everyone has unique gifts and creativity.

Who has not been stirred by quality music, theater, and other cultural expressions? They lift the spirit and bring the mind to a higher place. No wonder the Apostle Paul encouraged us to think on those things which are lovely. We can fill our homes with beautiful music, hang pictures that reflect God's goodness, and read material that reminds us of the loveliness of life. These influences will help us think uplifting thoughts and bring order to our minds.

Thinking What Is Admirable

Filling our minds with what is admirable includes thoughts containing good report. In other words, things spoken kindly and with goodwill toward others.

We certainly see enough evil reports—on every newscast, in the newspaper, and certainly on Coffee Row! Bad news travels fast. Gossipers spread stories, rumormongers seek the latest scoop, and shallow minds are filled with trash.

We can choose, however, to fill our thoughts with good news and spread wholesome words. Eleanor Roosevelt wrote, "Great minds discuss ideas; average minds discuss events; small minds discuss people."[20] Wouldn't it be wonderful if folks would include all the good news in their conversations? Let's not wait for someone else—we can be conveyors of happy words, encouraging remarks, good tidings, and cheerful reports.

Remember, what we think about is what we talk about. If we seek to think the best of others, our conversation will reflect wholesome, kind words. If people talk to us about others who aren't present, they'll also discuss us when we're absent.

> Remember, what we think about is what we talk about.

At our workplaces, or in daily contacts, we may be bombarded by talebearers spreading tidbits of hearsay. Refuse to ruminate on the bad news; rather, seek ways to disperse good reports.

Thinking What Is Excellent

Thinking on what is excellent includes virtuous thoughts. Excellence always signifies superior quality, high value, and great distinction. It represents our best and most valued achievements. Having excellence in our thoughts equals keeping our minds filled with the ideals related to everything virtuous.

The definition of virtue also alludes to strength, ability, and moral responsibility. When our minds are centered on Christ, our thoughts will include every good, life-giving purpose. These thoughts will even produce wisdom and vitality within us.

The Bible tells the story of Daniel, a Jewish youth who was taken captive from Judah to Babylon in 607 B.C. In spite of his captivity and extenuating circumstances, he determined to be a God-fearing man of integrity and excellence. Surrounded by all the glitter of Babylon, the Bible tells us in Daniel 1:8 that he *"resolved not to defile himself."*

When our minds are centred on Christ, our thoughts will include every good, life-giving purpose.

His fine character resulted in distinction and promotion. For seventy years, he held powerful political offices. His lifestyle of virtue and excellence was generated by a disciplined mind. Daniel 5:11–12 describes the man he had become:

There is a man in your kingdom who has the spirit of the holy gods in him. In the time of your father he was found to have insight and intelligence and wisdom like that of the gods...Daniel, whom the king called Belteshazzar, was found to have a keen mind and knowledge and understanding, and also the ability to interpret dreams, explain riddles and solve difficult problems.

God will honor integrity. Make the decision to meditate on thoughts of virtue and excellence. In Proverbs 2:7–12, we find God's promises for those who seek His wisdom:

He grants a treasure of good sense to the godly. He is their shield, protecting those who walk with integrity. He guards the paths of justice and protects those who are faithful to him. Then you will understand what is right, just, and fair, and you will know how to find the right course of action every time. For wisdom will enter your heart, and knowledge will fill you with joy. Wise planning will watch over you. Understanding will keep you safe. Wisdom will save you from evil people, from those whose speech is corrupt. (NLT)

Thinking What Is Praiseworthy

Finally, the Apostle Paul admonished us to meditate on what is wholesome and inspiring. This includes honor and praise to God, the recognition of human kindness and decency, as well as gratitude for every blessing.

Cultivate an attitude of gratitude.

Everyone needs reassurance. When we see the good people do, we should be quick to tell them. Words of encouragement should come from genuine thoughts of appreciation for others. We will inspire renewed courage when we sow seeds of thankfulness.

Cultivate an attitude of gratitude. Choose the positive perspective in every experience. Instead of dwelling on hurtful happenings, replay delightful occurrences and pleasing encounters. Discipline the memory to concentrate on past kindnesses, warm-hearted incidents, exciting events, and even amazing miracles. It is impossible to be depressed and thankful at the same time.

Melody Beattie once said,

> Gratitude unlocks the fullness of life. It turns what we have into enough, and more. It turns denial into acceptance, chaos to order, confusion to clarity. It can turn a meal into a feast, a house into a home, a stranger into a friend. Gratitude makes sense of our past, brings peace for today, and creates a vision for tomorrow.[21]

When we choose to meditate on that which is praiseworthy, our minds will have no room left for pessimism. We won't find happiness; happiness will find us.

As we habitually filter our thoughts by these eight godly values, optimism will pervade our minds with hope and cheer. By renewing our thought patterns according to these principles, our characters will be transformed. We will become reflections of the holiness of our Lord Jesus Christ.

Questions to Assist Practical Application

1. Have you deliberately replaced damaging thoughts with wholesome thoughts? What has been the fruit of positive thoughts in your life?

2. What are some occasions when you believed false assumptions?

3. Have you permitted noble, honorable, and honest thoughts to fill your mind? Have you been ensnared by habitual, impure thoughts? Do you desire to be free?

4. Describe some of your most beautiful, wholesome memories.

5. In what ways do you intend to attain excellence in your thought life?

6. List people for whom you are grateful. Have you ever expressed your thankfulness to them?

Challenge
*"Set your minds on things above,
not on earthly things."*
Colossians 3:2

chapter six
Receiving Transformation

Change your thoughts and you change your world.
Norman Vincent Peale[22]

*Whether you think you can,
or you think you can't—you're right.*
Henry Ford[23]

God transforms us by helping us change the way we think. Perhaps negative thought patterns have been a part of your life so long that they seem impossible to change. But there is hope. Don't give up. Start now. Every victory will bring new strength.

When a baby elephant is being trained, a chain around his neck is secured to a solid stake. The little pachyderm tugs, trying to escape. Eventually realizing the futility of the struggle, he submits to captivity.

As the elephant grows, he doesn't recognize his increasing strength. A chain around his neck attached to a relatively small block of wood or cement is sufficient to hold him captive. He has been trained since babyhood that he cannot get away. However, it is no longer the chain that holds him, but the mind that says, "I can never be free."

> *We can experience complete transformation by letting God's power help us change the way we think.*

Jesus paid the penalty to destroy the bondages in our lives. We can be liberated from evil habits, anger, unforgiveness, and bitterness. The prison doors are open; the chains have been loosed. We can be free if we want to be.

When we come to Jesus Christ, new life awaits us. Where we've come from isn't nearly as important as where we're going! T.W. Hunt wrote, "In the humanistic world-view we are what we have been. In the spiritual world-view we are what we are becoming."[24] The best is yet to come! We can experience complete transformation by letting God's power help us change the way we think.

Mere positive thinking ignores unpleasant thoughts, refusing to acknowledge or admit negative realities. However, Holy-Spirit-controlled thinking recognizes God's sovereign purpose in every human experience. In spite of heartbreaks, we find comfort and strength through Christ-centered thoughts.

Take the challenge to meet every thought with the positive affirmations of the Word of God. We can present our concerns to God in prayer, release them into His care, and receive His peace into our hearts and minds.

Patient Perseverance

We must be patient with ourselves if we slip back into old habits of negative thought. If we fail, voices of condemnation quickly berate and beat up on us. It's not the failures we must count, however, but the steady progress. We must continually monitor our thoughts as we reach for excellence. We'll succeed by taking one step at a time. Don't try to solve everything at once. Patient progress will produce permanent change.

Consistently choosing new ways of thinking will produce results.

Perseverance is necessary. Consistently choosing new ways of thinking will produce results. A Chinese proverb reminds us, "The most difficult obstacles can be overcome by simply taking one step at a time, but you *must keep on* stepping."

In the children's tale, a little train has to pull a large load up a steep grade. Approaching the hill, the small steam engine is filled with trepidation. Climbing, huffing and puffing, pulling with all its might, its wheels clicking, it begins to say, "I think I can, I think I can." Ever more slowly—but steadily—it chugged, "I think I can, I think I can," until it reached the summit. Then it clattered with joy, "I know I can, I know I can."

Tremendous potential is unleashed when we take the challenge to embrace impossibilities. Dare to reach beyond the habits of the past. Catch the vision of a renewed mind.

A large toad was sitting at the bottom of a deep rut. A man passing by saw him. He told the toad that he better get out of the rut or a truck could come along and squash him.

The old toad declared, "I can't. I tried, but I can't."

A short time later, another passerby admonished the toad to move before it was too late. Again the toad replied, "I can't. I tried, but I can't."

Later, the first man returned and discovered the toad sitting in the grass by the side of the road. He was so pleased and said to the toad, "I'm so glad you got out of the rut. But how did you do it, since you said you couldn't?"

"I couldn't," the toad replied, "but then a big truck came and I *had* to!"

Now is the time to make the choice to change the way we think. Determine to live free.

A humorous yarn is told of an inebriated man who staggered through a graveyard on his way home from the bar. In the dark of night, he tumbled into a freshly dug open grave. In his drunken state, he tried several times to climb out. Finally exhausted, he sat down in the corner of the pit.

Some minutes later, another intoxicated man fell into the same hole. He likewise struggled in vain to escape—unaware that the first man was quietly watching his efforts. After some moments, the voice of the first man commented in the darkness, "You'll never get out of here."

In a flash, the second man was out! It's surprising what can be accomplished when we have incentive!

As we patiently persevere, we will notice the difference. Gradually our renewed, wholesome thought patterns will bring positive change to our lives.

Proactive Perception

As we relax from the tension and stress of anger, fear, and anxiety, we become more receptive to bright and clear thinking. Fresh ideas and creative inspiration can flow into our minds. In Proverbs 8:12, the personification of Wisdom speaks, *"I, Wisdom, live together with good judgment. I know where to discover knowledge and discernment"* (NLT).

Holy-Spirit-controlled thinking releases the Lord's wisdom, making it available for us to bring His blessing to those around us. He can inspire ingenious ideas that create productivity. We can realize a new dimension of hopefulness, cheerfulness, and resourcefulness. A clear, optimistic mind becomes more articulate, imaginative, and innovative.

When we lift our thoughts away from self-centered and negative darkness, we see our circumstances from a totally different perspective. Hopelessness ebbs away in the light of faith-filled thought.

> *We have the authority to review our thoughts and evaluate them from the perspective of the grace God extends to us.*

Many years ago, a shoe company was hoping to expand. They sent representatives to Africa to explore the possibilities. One quickly sent back a telegram saying, "No potential, no one wears shoes." The other man, however, had a totally different perspective. His wire read, "Huge possibilities; everyone needs shoes!"

We must change our perception of who we are. We have tremendous value in the eyes of God. We are so precious to Him that He gave His only Son, Jesus, to die for us. We're full of untapped potential; we must see ourselves through the love-filled eyes of God. We have the authority to review all our thoughts and evaluate them from the perspective of the grace God extends to us.

Some thoughts we must choose to ignore. When negative, joy-sucking situations try to gain entry into our minds, we don't have to entertain them or come under their influence. We have the right to reject them. Let's rather choose to replay our blessings and victories.

As we refuse to be victims, we choose to proactively seek solutions. Instead of succumbing to despair, we use our minds to find innovative answers to problems. Instead of settling in for long, lonely pity parties, we decide to think of ways to succeed.

A great sense of humor is a wonderful gift. Sometimes we take ourselves far too seriously. It can be powerfully liberating to change our perspective and look on the funny side of life. It's healthy to learn to laugh at ourselves, to chuckle at amusing incidents, and to enjoy good, clean fun. A good belly laugh can heal the body and mind.

It is scientifically proven that laughter releases soothing, healing hormones. One article states:

> Laughter is a powerful antidote to stress, pain, and conflict. Nothing works faster or more dependably

to bring your mind and body back into balance than a good laugh. Humor lightens your burdens, inspires hopes, connects you to others, and keeps you grounded, focused, and alert.

With so much power to heal and renew, the ability to laugh easily and frequently is a tremendous resource for surmounting problems, enhancing your relationships, and supporting both physical and emotional health. Laughter relaxes the whole body, boosts the immune system, triggers the release of endorphins, and protects the heart.[25]

When we change our perspective, we think like winners. We dare to see ourselves from God's viewpoint. We think through problems, find answers, and actively engage in constructive solutions. Instead of being downhearted, grumpy, and critical, we experience laughter and joy.

Pursue the Prize

Continue to pursue excellent thoughts. The goal is worth the price. Aim for the highest. Choose the best. Reach for the finest. My father used to say, "It's better to aim for the stars and hit the woodpile. If you aim at the pile, you'll probably hit yourself in the foot!"

Receiving Transformation

A friend of mine has had to overcome many obstacles. She's an English-speaking black woman living in a white, French-speaking community. As a child, her family of eleven children lived in abject poverty—literally dependent on God to supply their daily bread. Racial prejudice intensified her struggle to obtain an education and steady employment.

After she married, although the complications seemed impossible, she was convinced God had sent her and her family to live and work in a financially depressed area. The mentality of the region was filled with hopelessness. There were few jobs. Most of the people had come to believe they'd never escape the cycle of poverty and addiction. Her husband even experienced serious and complicated health issues.

She began to preach the gospel, and then established a church. She became a pastor and slowly won the respect and hearts of the entire community. Under her leadership, the church has opened two senior care facilities and one home for Alzheimer's patients. Employment and compassion are being offered to many needy people. Both the local and provincial governments have been impacted by her steady, positive influence.

Although everything seemed stacked against her, she has turned great challenges into huge victories. The Lord has walked with her as she's made herself available. Her mindset has been Romans 8:31—*"If God is for us, who can be against us?"*

> Choose to reject poisonous thinking; permit positive thoughts to flourish.

Determine to make a difference. It starts by changing the way you think. Every day is a new opportunity. Choose to reject poisonous thinking; permit positive thoughts to flourish. Feed them with healthy, optimistic input, with productive, profitable ideas. Let your conversation and entertainment reflect beauty and virtue. This will continually remind you of your pursuit of excellence.

There are always hard times or difficulties. Everyone experiences setbacks and discouragements. However, we can choose to change the way we respond to them.

I once heard a story about an old farmer who had an old mule. One day, the mule fell into an old dry well. It was about three meters deep. When the farmer looked down and saw his mule, he had no idea how to get him out.

Finally, he decided the only solution was to get a large load of dirt and shovel it into the well. The mule was old and the well should have been filled long ago. He would bury the mule, fill the well, and both problems would be solved.

As he began to shovel dirt into the well, the mule brayed piteously. The farmer couldn't bear to look. With his back to the well, he continued his macabre work. The mule stopped making any sound. The old farmer brushed a tear as he thought of his faithful mule.

Suddenly, he saw the mule galloping across the field! What had happened? How had he gotten out of the well? The farmer inspected his work. As every shovel full of dirt had fallen on him, the old mule had shaken it off. He stepped on it and came up higher. By the time the well was filled, he simply walked away from a well-packed well!

When life throws its misery at us, we can be just like the mule: shake it off, step on it, and rise higher! It is our choice.

One personal encounter with Jesus Christ will alter the deepest parts of your identity. As you yield to Him, the power of the Holy Spirit will enable you to implement the principles of right thinking. He transforms *you*, empowering *you* to change the way you think.

Questions to Assist Practical Application

1. What practical actions will you take to maintain positive thought?

2. Are you patient with yourself? Can you laugh at yourself?

3. Do you have positive perceptions of yourself and your circumstances? Name individuals who have surmounted great difficulties by their positive choices.

4. What do you consider the greatest achievement in your life?

5. What choices are you making to create life-fulfilling consequences? Will your present habits of thought produce regret, or peace and satisfaction?

6. At the end of your life, how do you want to be remembered? Will your present thoughts and lifestyle produce an honorable memorial?

Challenge

"Therefore, since we are surrounded by such a great cloud of witnesses, let us throw off everything that hinders and the sin that so easily entangles, and let us run with perseverance the race marked out for us. Let us fix our eyes on Jesus, the author and perfecter of our faith, who for the joy set before him endured the cross, scorning its shame, and sat down at the right hand of the throne of God. Consider him who endured such opposition from sinful men, so that you will not grow weary and lose heart."

Hebrews 12:1–3

Conclusion

In his book, *Every Day a Friday*, Joel Osteen relates this story:

> John was ninety-two years old and blind, but he was just as sharp as could be when his wife, Eleanor, went to the Lord. He didn't feel he should live alone, so John decided to move into a nice seniors' home. On the morning of the move, he was up and fully dressed by 8:00 a.m. As always, the elderly gentleman looked impeccable, with his hair perfectly combed and his face neatly shaven. A cab picked him up and took him to the seniors' home. John arrived early, as was his habit, and waited more than an hour before a young aide, Miranda, came to show him to his new room. As John maneuvered his walker through the hallways, Miranda described his room in great detail. She said

sunlight came in through a big window, and there was a comfortable couch, and a nice desk area.

Right in the middle of her description, John interrupted her and said, "I love it. I love it. I love it."

Miranda laughed and said, "Sir, we're not there yet. You haven't seen it. Hold on just a minute, and I'll show it to you."

John said, "No, you don't have to show it to me. Whether I like my room or not doesn't depend on how the furniture is arranged. It depends on how my mind is arranged. Happiness is something you decide ahead of time."[26]

* * *

Our minds are the garden in which we nurture our thoughts. The fruit is revealed in our attitudes, emotions, words, actions, and health. Every outward expression in our lives is produced first in our minds.

Personal responsibility for our thoughts is one of the most important lessons we can learn. What we do is a reflection of who we are, and who we are is the result of what we choose to think.

There is power in positive thinking. However, there's a dimension far greater than merely being optimistic: a personal relationship with Jesus Christ. God's Word, the name of Jesus, the blood of Jesus, and gratefulness are effective spiritual tools to bring about profound transformation. We can depend on His supernatural resources to work in us, producing Holy-Spirit-controlled thinking.

It is our choice to recognize and refuse life-damaging thoughts. We don't need to be controlled by the poisonous toxins of fear, anger, and self-centeredness. We can refuse polluted thinking.

We can experience the liberation and restoration of positive, Holy-Spirit-centered thought patterns. Filling our minds with the quality values of integrity, justice, and purity produces virtuous and excellent character. This transformation will bring healing, joy, and peace. We will discover hearts of winners—and the winners will be us.

The Gift of Salvation

If you've never given your life to Christ, I earnestly urge you to surrender to Him today. According to Romans 3:23, *"all have sinned and fall short of the glory of God."*

The Bible tells us that peace with God is received by turning to Him from our sins. In Romans 10:9–10, 13, we read:

> *That if you confess with your mouth, "Jesus is Lord," and believe in your heart that God raised him from the dead, you will be saved. For it is with your heart that you believe and are justified, and it is with your mouth that you confess and are saved… "Everyone who calls on the name of the Lord will be saved."*

Choose A Changed Mind

You can receive His life now by repentance and faith. Pray this simple prayer:

> Lord, I know I have sinned. I believe You are the Son of God and that You died on the cross to forgive my sins. I believe You have risen from the dead and have the power to give me a transformed life. Please forgive me, change my heart, and set me free. I surrender the control of my will to You. Help me to follow You. In Jesus' name. Amen.

Read the Bible and pray every day. Find others who love Jesus who can help you follow Him. With your hand in the hand of Jesus, you can choose a changed mind and a new life in Him.

Endnotes

1 Dr. David Jeremiah, "You Are Not What You Think You Are, But What You Think, You Are," *LightSource*, 7 April 2013 (http://www.lightsource.com/ministry/turning-point/you-are-not-what-you-think-you-are-but-what-you-think-you-are-337537.html).

2 Blaise Pascal, "Thought Quotes," *BrainyQuote*, 6 August 2013 (http://www.brainyquote.com/quotes/keywords/thought_4.html).

3 Author Unknown, "Hospital Window," *Moral Stories*, 13 September 2008 (http://academictips.org/blogs/moral-tale-hospital-window/).

4 Marlo Sollitto, "Sick with Worry: How Thoughts Affect Your Health," *Agingcare.com*, 10 June 2013 (http://www.agingcare.com/Articles/health-problems-caused-by-stress-143376.htm).

5 Dr. Caroline Leaf, *Who Switched off My Brain?* (Southlake, TX: Inprov, 2009), 20, 36. Revised edition.

6 Louisa May Alcott, "My Little Kingdom," *Cordula's Web*, 10 June 2013 (http://www.cordula.ws/poems/kingdom.html).

7 James Lane Allen, "Quotable Quote," *Goodreads*, 10 June 2013 (http://www.goodreads.com/quotes/431848-the-man-who-sows-wrong-thoughts-and-deeds-and-prays).

8 Albert Schweitzer, "Man must cease attributing…" *QuotationsBooks*, 9 August 2013 (http://quotationsbook.com/quote/34245/#sthash.q6d7jQbk.dpbs).

9 Ralph Waldo Emerson, "Sow a thought…" *QuotationsBook*, 10 June 2013 (http://quotationsbook.com/quote/10741/#sthash.sgxgboU3.dpbs).

10 Dr. Caroline Leaf, *Who Switched Off My Brain?* (Southland, TX: Inprov, 2009), 99. Revised edition.

11 Joseph M. Scriven, "Joseph M. Scriven," *Wikipedia*, 11 June 2013 (https://en.wikipedia.org/wiki/Joseph_M._Scriven).

12 Cicero, "Cicero Quotes," *SearchQuotes*, 10 June 2013 (http://www.searchquotes.com/quotation/A_thankful_heart_is_not_only_the_greatest_virtue,_but_the_parent_of_all_the_other_virtues./294401/).

Endnotes

13 Author Unknown, "Thank God for Dirty Dishes", *Scrapbook.com*, 10 June 2013 (http://www.scrapbook.com/poems/doc/1795/53.html).

14 John C. Maxwell, *Everyone Communicates, Few Connect* (Nashville, TN: Thomas Nelson, 2009), 224–225.

15 Marcus Aurelius, "The happiness of your life…" *BrainyQuote*. 10 June 2013 (http://www.brainyquote.com/quotes/quotes/m/marcusaure121534.html).

16 John Dryden, "John Dryden Quotes," *Goodquotes.com*, 10 June 2013 (http://www.goodquotes.com/quote/john-dryden/anger-will-never-disappear-so-long-as).

17 Dr. Caroline Leaf, *Who Switched off My Brain?* (Southlake, TV: Inprov, 2009), 87. Revised edition.

18 Charles R. Swindoll, "The secret of living…" *BrainyQuote*, 10 June 2013 (http://www.brainyquote.com/quotes/quotes/c/charlesrs130092.html).

19 Robert H. Schuller, "Thought Quotes," *BrainyQuote*, 6 August 2013 (http://www.brainyquote.com/quotes/keywords/thought.html).

20 Eleanor Roosevelt, "Great minds discuss…" *BrainyQuote*, 10 June 2013 (http://www.brainyquote.com/quotes/quotes/e/eleanorroo385439.html).

21 Melody Beattie, "Quotes," *Goodreads*, 10 June 2013 (http://www.goodreads.com/author/quotes/4482.Melody_Beattie).

22 Norman Vincent Peale, "Norman Vincent Peale Quotes," *BrainyQuote*, 10 June 2013 (http://www.brainyquote.com/quotes/authors/n/norman_vincent_peale.html).

23 Henry Ford, "Quotes About Thinking," *Goodreads*, 6 August 2013 (http://www.goodreads.com/quotes/tag/thinking).

24 T.W. Hunt, *The Mind of Christ: The Transforming Power of Thinking His Thoughts* (Nashville, TN: Broadman & Holman Publishers, 1995), 156.

25 Melinda Smith and Jeanne Segal, "Laughter Is the Best Medicine," *Helpguide.org*, 10 June 2013 (http://www.helpguide.org/life/humor_laughter_health.htm).

26 Joel Osteen, *Every Day a Friday* (New York, NY: FaithWords, 2011), 3.

Also authored by Anita Pearce:
Choose to Live Life
ISBN-13: 978-1-77069-741-6

Our character and core values are results of our choices. We have the tremendous capacity to determine who we will be. We cannot always control our circumstances, but we do have the power to decide our reactions and attitudes in response to them. It is that ability which enables us not just to survive, but also to thrive in seemingly impossible situations-to turn lemons into lemonade. This book presents the challenge to choose to follow Christ and live life passionately.

Products available from Inspiration Ministries:

BOOKS:
Above the Storm
Joy in the Journey
Choose to Live Life

MUSIC CDS:
Grace
Collection of Favorites
The Timeless Prize
Mercy
He Loved Me Enough

For a complete catalogue of Anita`s music, CDs, DVDs, and other ministry information, please visit her website at
www.inspirationministries.net
and order yours today!